M000195042

For:

_____

With Love From:

_____

I always thank God for you.

1 CORINTHIANS 1:4

Editor: Molly Detweiler
Compiler: Doris Rikkers
Project Manager: Jessica Start
Design: Chris Gannon
Illustration: Lyn Boyer Nelles

Printed in China
00 01 02/HK/5 4 3 2 1

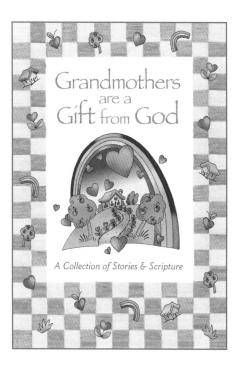

Grandmothers
are a
Gift from God

A Collection of Stories & Scripture

Zondervan *Gifts*

We have a gift for inspiration™

May the LORD bless you…

all the days of your life…

and may you live to see

your children's children.

PSALM 128:5–6

A child is born. But this is not just any birth or any child. This birth establishes a new generation. This child signifies the beginning of the future. This new baby brings a transformation, changing an ordinary woman into an extraordinary one.

This one little life will make all the difference in the world—for this child will call you Grandma!

What is a Grandmother?

A grandmother is a combination of work-worn hands, after a lifetime of toil, a loving heart, and endless stories of the days when her family was young.

Grandmothers wear old age with dignity and composure. You don't notice what grandmothers wear, you only see the love and tenderness in her face as she cuddles her youngest grandchild.

Grandmothers have spent a whole lifetime cooking meals that statisticians
would be unable to record, keeping
house, helping neighbors, drying the tears of the
past generation as well as the present, and praying
that she may be allowed to go on doing it all for a
few more years.

Grandmothers have run the whole gamut of
human emotions—joy, defeat, success, failure,
heartache, sorrow, and perhaps tragedy. They
have come through with the wisdom and tranquil-
ity endowed to those whose tears have been
replaced by the calm acceptance and quiet out-
look of those who have weathered life's battles.

The nicest possible place to hear a story is in
Grandmother's lap. Giants and ogres hold no ter-
rors when you are held in the warmth and love of
a grandmother with your head pillowed on her
shoulder.

Grandmothers can always be
counted on to produce
sweets, cookies and candies that
seem to taste nicer from her than
from anyone else.

Grandmothers just don't believe that their grandchildren have any faults. They can be relied upon to champion the underdog and lost causes. When a chap is in trouble for not washing behind the ears, she will console him by telling him that his dad was almost *nine* before he overcame that problem.

Grandmothers can soothe an unruly, weeping young boy or girl just by rocking them on her lap and crooning in a soft voice.

Grandmothers give the impression of being all wisdom and love whether in giving help or advice to a neighbor or making a hurt finger better with a kiss.

ELIZABETH FAYE

*Pleasant words are a honeycomb,
sweet to the soul and healing to the bones.*

PROVERBS 16:24

*As God's chosen people, holy and dearly loved,
clothe yourselves with compassion, kindness,
humility, gentleness and patience.*

COLOSSIANS 3:12

Love is patient, love is kind.

1 CORINTHIANS 13:4

Though gray be your hair
With little to part
This does not denote
The age of your heart.

MICHAEL FRANKLIN ELLIS

How amusing are the answers people of different ages give to "How old are you?" A youngster will say, "I'm five-and-a-half and three months." A teenager: "I'm almost sixteen" (when she is actually just fifteen). A woman nearing middle age: "I'm in my forties." While Grandma proudly answers, "Eighty next birthday."

It seems you have to be young enough or old enough to be proud of your age!

Wrinkles are only the by-paths of many smiles, and some tears; gray hair is the silver-dust of the stars; and growing gracefully slower of step is only walking nearer to God.

LAVETTA HUMMEL

Gray hair is a crown of splendor;
it is attained by a righteous life.

PROVERBS 16:31

The LORD will guide you always;
he will satisfy your needs ...
and will strengthen your frame.

ISAIAH 58:11

Is not wisdom found among the aged?
Does not long life bring understanding?

JOB 12:12

The Lord will renew your life
and sustain you in your old age.

RUTH 4:15

A garden of love grows in
my grandmother's heart.

A grandma's love
is a glimpse of heaven.

A few days before my grandmother died, I was able to speak with her on the telephone. She was in a hospital in Brussels, Belgium. "Oh, Christopher," she said. "Oh, Christopher." She wasn't weeping. She wasn't in pain. As she simply repeated my name, all the memories of my grandmother flew out through the international telephone cable: her singing French songs about my grandfather riding a horse, her laughter when my sister Anne and I performed a circus in the attic with our cat, Tiger Lily. My grandmother: her perfume, her worn slippers, her housedress and brown stockings. She liked butterscotch and port and ice cream and card games, and she loved me.

CHRISTOPHER DE VINCK

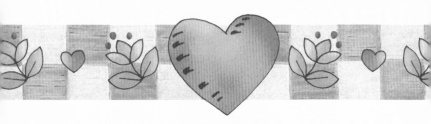

My grandma likes to play with God,
They have a kind of game.
She plants the garden full of seeds,
He sends the sun and rain.

She likes to sit and talk with God
And knows he is right there.
She prays about the whole wide world,
Then leaves us in his care.

ANN JOHNSON (AGE EIGHT)
The Lutheran Standard

The righteous will flourish like a palm tree,
they will grow like a cedar of Lebanon;
planted in the house of the LORD,
they will flourish in the courts of our God.
They will still bear fruit in old age,
they will stay fresh and green,
proclaiming, "The LORD is upright;
he is my Rock."

PSALM 92:12–15

Lord, you have been our dwelling place
throughout all generations.
Before the mountains were born or you
brought forth the earth and the world,
from everlasting to everlasting you are God.

PSALM 90:1–2

We Thank Thee

A little sunshine, a little rain,
A little loss and a little gain,
Courage to walk the unknown road,
Strength to carry the tiring load,
Blossoming flowers and beauteous trees,
Singing birds—for all of these
We thank thee, God.

For memories of voices sweet,
Of beauty fresh and eager feet
That will not run again our way,
For all the joys of yesterday,
For vision to undo the bars
Of doubting night and see the stars,
We thank thee, God.

ADELAIDE R. KEMP

*How much better to get wisdom than gold,
to choose understanding rather than silver!*

PROVERBS 16:16

*Let us not love with words or tongue but
with actions and in truth.*

1 JOHN 3:18

*The LORD is good to those
whose hope is in him.*

LAMENTATIONS 3:25

The wisdom of a grandmother is in her patience. Her quiet silence induces a confession of guilt in less than three minutes.

DWR

Any grandmother can tell you what's new in people. And she has pictures to go with her wonderful story.

HERALD, AZUSA, CALIFORNIA

One of the most influential handclasps is that of a grandchild around the finger of a grandparent.

GAZETTE, HIGH BRIDGE, NEW JERSEY

The greatest gift a grandmother can give her grandchildren is her faith.

My grandmother makes me think that God is her best friend. I hope I can know him that way too.

Even when I am old and gray,
do not forsake me, O God, till I
declare your power to the next generation,
your might to all who are to come.

PSALM 71:18

Grandma didn't have much education, and she knew nothing about theology, but she sure knew how to love. For more than fifty years she taught Sunday school to two-year-olds. When Grandma died at eighty-five, the church was filled for her funeral. Many stood to pay tribute to her living demonstration of God's love. A lot of people have personal relationships with God because Grandma loved their little children. Her's was a simple faith—childlike, really. Yet I wonder if Grandma, in all her simplicity, wasn't a more effective evangelist than the world's greatest preachers.

BETTY SOUTHARD AND JAN STOOP

I helped a little child to see
That God had made a willow tree,
And God became more real to me.
I tried to lead a child through play
To grow more Christlike every day,
And I myself became that way.
I joined a little child in prayer,
And as we bowed in worship there,
I felt anew God's loving care.
Thank you, dear Lord;
How grandly true:
By guiding children, we find you!

Growing up in Kansas, my sisters and I needed only to cross the street to go to Grandmother's. She lived in the old Victorian where my father and his six sisters had been raised. I sat on the same front porch, ate at the same table, played in the same attic, slept on the same sleeping porch, explored the same fruit cellar, swung under the same tree, and swiped the same soft ginger cookies my dad had thrived on. My cousins—some from as far away as Illinois or California—adored Grandmother and her cookies, too, but I believed the proprietary rights were mine.

FRANCES WEAVER

Distance cannot diminish
a grandmother's love.

Although we lived a continent apart and
rarely saw each other, I always adored my
grandmother. I knew that since I was her
only granddaughter I was equally adored.
Even now, the highest compliment my
mother can pay me is, "Your grandmother
would be so proud of you."

CAROLINE BLAUWKAMP

God gives strength to the weary
and increases the power of the weak. ...
Those who hope in the LORD
will renew their strength.
They will soar on wings like eagles;
they will run and not grow weary,
they will walk and not be faint.

ISAIAH 40:29, 31

After a day of watching the grandchildren,
the Lord renews our strength in a very
practical way—he lets us send them home.

He does not lead me year by year
        nor even day by day.
But step by step my path unfolds;
        my Lord directs my way.

Tomorrow's plans I do not know,
        I only know this minute:
But he will say, "This is the way,
        by faith now walk ye in it."

And I am glad that it is so;
        today's enough to bear,
And when tomorrow comes, his grace
        shall far exceed its care.

What need to worry then or fret;
        the God who gave his Son
Holds all the moments in his hand,
        and gives them one by one.

BARBARA C. RYBERG

Each year my Grandmother Inez planted tulips in her flower garden and looked forward to their springtime beauty with childlike anticipation. Under her loving guardianship, they sprang up each April faithfully, and she was never disappointed. But she said the real flowers that decorated her life were her grandchildren.

LYNETTE CURTIS

The reason God made grandmas is they are sweet, they comfort you when you're down—and most of all—because they love you.

BREANAH SHANTEL GRAY, AGE 8

A grandmother doesn't have to do anything.
You just need to know she's somewhere
thinking of you.

Granddaughters change your priorities. If they
want to play peek-a-boo, dinner will have to wait.

CAROL VELTMAN

I like to think of the hand of my grandmother.
She would bring her hand down in the darkness
as she stood over my bed before I slept. I was
ten. She was eighty. She'd place her hand on my
head and offer a blessing in Flemish: "A cross
and a sleep well," she'd whisper.

CHRISTOPHER DE VINCK

The one thing I learned from my grandmother was how to play Tarzan. My brother and I would each spend a week with Grandmother during the summer. Grandmother would find things for us to do. We had picnics, we played with the dog, we went on nature hikes, we fished in the pond, and, oh yeah, we would swing over the brook on the vine that hung there. After all, who wants to walk home in wet shoes?

REGINA HUGHES

Grandmas Are a Gift from God

They come down from heaven in airplanes.

They serve tea and special cookies
in the afternoon.

They write real letters on fancy paper that
show up in my mailbox.

They live in places where I can
swim in the winter.

They don't ask—they just hug.

They love me the way I am.

They arrive when a new baby does.

They make me laugh.

They give me presents wrapped
in paper and ribbons.

They listen.

33

Every summer we would visit my grandmother at the Jersey shore. She would load us up with love and our favorite foods. French toast for breakfast. Fried Taylor's ham with melted cheese on hard rolls for lunch. Pot roast for dinner and three desserts afterwards. In between there were Tastykakes and Wise potato chips—treats we couldn't get in Michigan. It's good we swam and jumped waves all day—we never gained weight.

MARK RIKKERS

Recipe for a
Happy Day

1 cup of friendly words
2 cups of understanding
4 heaping tablespoons of time
A pinch of warm personality
A dash of humor
Mix well and
serve in generous portions.

Where Did You Come From?

Where did you come from, Baby dear?
Out of everywhere into here.

Where did you get your eyes so blue?
Out of the sky as I came through.

What makes the light in them sparkle and spin?
Some of the starry spikes left in.

Where did you get that little tear?
I found it waiting when I got here.

What makes your forehead so smooth and high?
A soft hand stroked it as I went by.

What makes your cheek like a warm white rose?

36

I saw something better than anyone knows.

Whence that three-corner'd smile of bliss?
Three angels gave me at once a kiss.

Where did you get this pearly ear?
God spoke, and it came out to hear.

Where did you get those arms and hands?
Love made itself into hooks and bands.

Feet, whence did you come, you darling things?
From the same box as the cherubs' wings.

How did they all come just to be you?
God thought of me, and so I grew.

But how did you come to us, you dear?
God thought of you, and so I am here.

GEORGE MACDONALD

How much better is the woman who trusts in God. She can regard the past as part of God's plan for her life. She can enjoy her family, her home, her entire life now because she knows God will add to her everything he wants her to have.

BARBARA BUSH

My grandma taught me all kinds of things just by my being around her when I was younger. She loved gardening, crocheting, baking, and sewing. She always had beautifully polished nails even though she worked in the garden. She wore lovely lace-topped nightgowns and she smelled so sweet. But best of all, she always said to me, "Bless your heart."

AMY PETERMAN

Grandmothers are the people who
take delight in hearing babies breathing
into the telephone.

PAM BROWN

If nothing is going well,
call your grandmother.

ITALIAN PROVERB

*Children's children are a crown to the aged,
and parents are the pride of their children.*

PROVERBS 17:6

In what way are grandchildren the crown of the elderly? In Bible times it was the exception rather than the rule for a man or a woman to live to see the second generation. Too many wars, diseases, and famines took lives at a relatively young age. To be able to see one's grandchildren was a sign of a special blessing from God. It was like being crowned by God; it meant being a winner with the Lord.

Being a grandparent is common today, though, isn't it? But don't ever take it for granted! Every grandchild born today signifies God's special love. It means God is faithful to his promises. It means God is blessing us today with extended lifespans. Thank God for that blessing.

There's no place like home—
except Grandma's!

Grandma's home is her grandchildren's second
home, a sort of security blanket they can
escape to when the world is unfriendly.

JANET LANESE

Show me your ways, O L<small>ORD</small>,
teach me your paths;
guide me in your truth and teach me,
for you are God my Savior,
and my hope is in you all day long.

<small>PSALM 25:4–5</small>

Praise the L<small>ORD</small>, all you nations;
extol him, all you peoples.
For great is his love toward us, and the
faithfulness of the L<small>ORD</small> endures forever.

<small>PSALM 117:1–2</small>

God is love.
Whoever lives in love lives in God,
and God in him.

<small>1 JOHN 4:16</small>

Grandmas Are Special Because ...

They know how to find information in a book encyclopedia, not on a computer.

They read my favorite books again and again and again.

They talk to God about me.

They visit my school.

They know which day is my birthday.

They don't make a big deal about how
I wear my hair.

They don't use e-mail, but that's okay.

They let me make a mess in the kitchen.

They know how to make tuna casserole
        from cans, not a box.

They sit down at the table to eat dinner.

My grandmother was a matriarch to the family and community and a moral compass to all. Even though she was confined to her rocking chair because of rheumatism, she had a vital interest in the lives of all those around her and could keep in touch since our homes were all within eyesight of hers. We grandchildren stopped in almost daily to "report in," which kept us on the "straight and narrow," living up to her moral and social expectations. We did not mind this supervision because we knew she genuinely cared about us. She added stability, wisdom, and tradition to our lives.

DAWN ANSPAUGH

A heart at peace gives life to the body.

PROVERBS 14:30

A gentle answer turns away wrath.

PROVERBS 15:1

The plans of the LORD stand firm forever, the purposes of his heart through all generations.

PSALM 33:11

Do not let your grandmother get old before you write down her recipes.

ANONYMOUS

Among my fondest memories of growing up in a small, central Texas farming-and-ranching community in the forties and fifties were sharing a dishpan full of popcorn with my mother and daddy and brothers, spending lazy summer days on the farm—and my grandmother, Pearl Watson, baking tea cakes in her wood cookstove. (How she knew how many sticks of wood to put in that stove to get 350 degrees I'll never know!) My grandmother always made them by the sacksful and we could eat to our heart's, or stomach's, content. Even today my eighty-eight-year-old grandmother still bakes up dozens of her tea cakes, though not in a woodstove, and they are everybody's favorite! But somehow it's not just the tea cakes themselves, but the warmth their very mention creates, even among the third and fourth generations.

VERDELL DAVIS

During the Depression my Grandmom invited neighbors on Saturday evenings for her potato pancakes. The pancakes and applesauce were made from potatoes and apples from the garden and eggs from the hen house. She'd make them by huge dishpansful and sometimes spend three or four hours frying as people came in the door.

PAT BURGER

My grandmother made the best rice pudding in the whole world. Unfortunately, like the rest of her recipes, it was in her head, not in a recipe book. Thus I spent years combing the world for the perfect rice pudding like Grandmother made. A few years ago I found a recipe which delivers what it promises.

JUDITH MARKHAM

Grandmothers are people who keep pictures of their grandchildren up on the walls, even if they don't match the decor.

My grandmother knows about everything I do—the good stuff and the bad. But she only remembers the good stuff.

Grandmothers have the time to stay at the park just a little longer, even when it's lunchtime.

*"I will make you the everlasting pride and
the joy of all generations," says the LORD.*

ISAIAH 60:15

*Posterity will serve him; future generations will
be told about the Lord.
They will proclaim his righteousness
to a people yet unborn.*

PSALM 22:30–31

*Paul wrote to Timothy, "I have been reminded
of your sincere faith, which first lived in your
grandmother Lois and in your mother Eunice
and, I am persuaded, now lives in you also."*

2 TIMOTHY 1:5

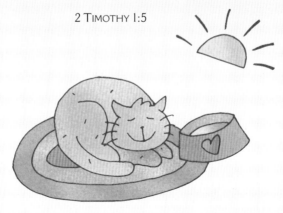

I Love My Grandma Because ...

She thinks I can do anything.

She doesn't want me to change.

She likes me no matter what.

She remembers my accomplishments
    and forgets my mistakes.

She doesn't yell.

She buys me clothes for back to school.

She has a big flowerpot full of sand
for me to play in.

She keeps special toys in the closet.

She lets me play the piano,
even when I don't know how.

She likes to be silly.

A Quiet Heart

O Lord, give me a quiet heart—
    So oft my heart is filled with fear;
I need the peace Thou canst impart;
    I need to feel that Thou art near.

Help me to walk by faith each day.
    Though shadows hide the path from
    view;
Give me a quiet heart, I pray
    To trust Thee as Thou bid'st me do.

I cannot see the journey's end,
	I know not what lies just ahead;
But, oh, I have a Heav'nly Friend
	Who knows the path my feet must tread.

So now, my heart, be still and trust,
	Although thou canst not see the way:
For He who formed thee from the dust
	Wilt lead thee on from day to day.

A quiet heart—a quiet heart,
	From which are banished doubts and fears;
O Lord, give me a quiet heart
	That trusts Thee for the coming years.

W.M. NIENHUIS

Our grandchildren accept us for ourselves, without rebuke or effort to change us, as no one in our entire lives has ever done.

RUTH GOODE

Age does not protect you from love. But love, to some extent, protects you from age.

JEANNE MOREAU

A grandmother is someone to run to when things aren't going so well at home.

My grandmother lived only three blocks from my house. Whenever my mother was fed up with either me or one of my four brothers, we would run over to see Grandma. She never asked why we were there. She just offered us sugar cookies and 7-Up and let us sit at the kitchen table with her for a while.

BILL RIKKERS

Not only is Nana my best friend, she's the smartest person in my family. My mother told me that it only took Nana one semester of college to hook grandpa and get her M.R.S. degree.

NICHOLAS (AGE TEN)

My grandma tells me she keeps the family skeletons in the closet, but I've looked and looked and still can't find them.

SARAH (AGE FIVE)

Home is where I hope to stay. I hope to be here when any of the children or grandchildren need me. From my vantage point I can look back on circumstances involving our children, situations I once felt were hopeless, only to see in disbelief and amazement as God brought order out of chaos, light out of darkness.

I will follow their struggles with peace in my heart. Battles may be lost, but God will win out in the end. We gave them to him, each one uniquely loved, each as dear as the other: our most treasured possessions. As each little family builds its nest, I shall be watching with interest and love, concern at times, but concern under-girded with confidence, knowing God is in control.

RUTH BELL GRAHAM

Know therefore that the L<small>ORD</small> your God is God;
he is the faithful God, keeping his covenant
of love to a thousand generations of those who
love him and keep his commands.

<small>DEUTERONOMY 7:9</small>

Do not forget my teaching,
but keep my commands in your heart,
for they will prolong your life many years
and bring you prosperity.

<small>PROVERBS 3:1–2</small>

Because my parents were both from Belgium, because my grandmother spent many summers with us, and because I had completed four successful years of French in high school, I signed up for French 1 in the fall of my freshman year in college. But I never learned any French in school. The only reason I could speak the language at all was because my grandmother insisted that I speak with her in French. I had the vocabulary of a six-year-old Belgian child and a grandmother who loved to play cards in the kitchen.

CHRISTOPHER DE VINCK

Lord, give me patience when wee hands
Tug at me with their small demands.
Give me gentle and smiling eyes;
Keep my lips from hasty replies.
Let not weariness, confusion, or noise
Obscure my vision of life's fleeting joys.

There's a special place in a child's heart that only a grandmother's love can fill.

The greatest thing about being a grandma is that my grandchildren don't see my age; they only know my love.

CAROL VELTMAN

All grandmothers like letters. Even if they just consist of a squiggle and a dirty finger mark.

PAM BROWN

By the time I was old enough to go to school, I assumed I would one day be an old lady like my grandmother. It was my intention to be exactly like her, but if Grandmother Allison and I could stand side by side today, the only similarity would be our weight. She was a hefty, well-corseted woman. So am I.

FRANCES WEAVER

My best friend, Nellie, had the perfect grand-mother. When we were about eight years old, we would visit Nellie's grandmother on the farm. She was a small, thin woman with gray hair that she wore in a bun. She would tell us stories of when she was a little girl. Best of all, she would let me help her pluck the dead chickens. (Nellie hated that job.) Pulling the white feathers out was such fun.

BEPPIE SCHROEDER

Grandmas teach you fractions better than anybody. They use blocks of chocolate. And they let you eat the sums when you're finished.

PAM BROWN

Grandma and I would sit and talk about heaven. She talked mostly about seeing Grandpa again. And her baby girl. Then we would discuss it. Would she still be a baby or grown now? And do you know what we decided? We decided heaven is how you want it.

Grandmothers are about twenty inside.
Sometimes six.

PAM BROWN

The nicest compliment one grandmother ever
received: "Grandma, I'll be glad when I'm as old
as you are, so I'll have as much fun as you do."

Grandmothers will laugh at all your jokes, and
they even have some of their own.
But they will not tell you dumb jokes
like lots of grown people tell.

A good laugh is sunshine in a house.

WILLIAM MAKEPEACE THACKERAY

Live in the sunshine of today and not in the shadows of yesterday.

A Sunday school teacher had been teaching the Bible verse "Draw nigh to God, and he will draw nigh to you" (James 4:8). When Charles, one of her students, got home, he happily repeated his memory verse to Grandmother—his own version: "Draw a line unto me, and I will draw a line unto you."

Grandma Always Makes Me Feel Good

She thinks I'm smarter than I really am.

She laughs at my knock-knock jokes—even the old ones.

She makes me feel like a grown-up.

She tells me funny stories of when she was little.

She sits down with me to talk.

She thinks I'm clever.

She shows off only the best pictures of me.

She tells me she misses me.

She buys me things that Mom says are too expensive.

She has an endless supply of kisses.

Every child needs
at least one grandmother.

I wish every frightened, lonely, sick,
bewildered child in the world had a
grandmother to run to.

PAM BROWN

You can never have enough grand-mothers. And grandmothers don't have to be related to you. When I was little, we had elderly neighbors living next door to us. Gert would invite me and my brother over to have cookies or to sit and talk on the front porch. Corine loved watching us play from her kitchen window. She would pay us for any small task we did for her. They both always remembered us on our birthdays and Christmas. It was like having two grandmothers right next door.

MARK RIKKERS

Someone Needs You

If you're feeling low and worthless,
There seems nothing you can do,
Just take courage and remember
There is someone needing you.

You were created for a purpose,
For a part in God's great Plan;
Bear ye one another's burdens,
So fulfill Christ's law to man.

If perhaps in bed you're lying,
You can smile or press the hand
Of the one who tells his story.
He will know you understand.

There are many sad and lonely,
And discouraged, not a few,
Who a little cheer are needing,
And there's someone needing you.

Someone needs your faith and courage,
Someone needs your love and prayer,
Someone needs your inspiration,
Thus to help their cross to bear.

Do not think your work is ended,
There is much that you can do,
And as long as you're on earth,
There is someone needing you.

SUSIE B. MARR

My own grandparents passed away before I was born, so I adopted a grandma about seven years ago when she moved into an assisted living center right next door to my apartment complex.

My adopted grandma's name is Jane, and she is beautiful, inside and out. I love to visit her. Just like any good grandmother, she has all of those special treats: candy in the candy dishes and ice cream in the freezer. She has my picture on her nightstand. She wants to know how everything in my life is going. She calls me special names like "darling," "angel," or "sweetheart." I love her words of wisdom and her stories of all of her life experiences. I have so much fun hearing about her many travel adventures, her favorite shows at the theater and the latest news of her children and grandchildren. I get a big smile when I think about her.

Our relationship is such a precious gift to me. I thank God for putting her in my life and giving me a grandmother to love.

PATTI MATTHEWS

Grandma's Prayer

I pray that, risen from the dead,
I may in glory stand—
A crown, perhaps, upon my head,
But a needle in my hand.

I've never learned to sing or play,
So let no harp be mine;
From birth unto my dying day,
Plain sewing's been my line.

Therefore, accustomed to the end
To plying useful stitches,
I'll be content if asked to mend
The little angels' breeches.

When everything has sagged and you're feeling ready for the scrap yard, along come the grandchildren and hand you back your youth in a fancy box. Come on, Grandma— get on your feet. You are starting all over again.

PAM BROWN

Praise the LORD, O my soul,
and forget not all his benefits—
who satisfies your desires with good things
so that your youth is renewed like the eagle's.

PSALM 103:2, 5

The LORD is my shepherd,
I shall not be in want.
He makes me lie down in green pastures,
he leads me beside quiet waters,
he restores my soul.

PSALM 23:1–3

Praise be to the God and Father of our Lord
Jesus Christ! In his great mercy he has given us
new birth into a living hope through the resur-
rection of Jesus Christ.

1 PETER 1:3

A hug does not require words.
In fact, there is no word
that can replace the emotion
of a hug.

TOM POTTS

Upon hearing of an upcoming visit from Grandmother, my siblings and I would become lost somewhere between euphoria and exuberance. Hardly able to contain ourselves from the sheer excitement of her pending arrival, we would make up chants and songs about "Grandma's coming" and sing them aloud and dance.

When grandma finally arrived, her immediate act of love would be to say, "Come here, little girls, and give me some sugar." The sugar she was referring to was not of the normal sort but kisses we were to plant on various parts of her face. She'd then proceed to pinch our noses and cheeks. Then she would give us the grandest hugs with kisses. From these hugs, I knew in my heart that I was greatly loved by my grandma.

PATRICIA GAINES

I Love Visiting Grandma Because ...

She lets me run in the house.

She collects sand dollars from the sea and makes them white.

She lets me sleep overnight at her house.

She makes Mickey Mouse waffles from scratch, not the kind from the freezer.

She plays games with me.

She takes naps when I do.

She makes meat that's easy to chew.

She listens to me read.

She lets me drink soda pop.

She lets me read in bed way past my bedtime.

I am still confident of this:
I will see the goodness of the LORD
in the land of the living.
Wait for the LORD;
be strong and take heart
and wait for the LORD.

PSALM 27:13–14

Everything my grandma cooked seemed to always taste better than my mother's cooking. My grandma wasn't much on recipe books, but she always knew the right amount of ingredients to use to make her dishes taste the best. She was born in the South in the state of Mississippi, so she had a flair for southern cooking. The grits always tasted better when Grandma made them. So did the sweet potato pie, the cornbread, and the chicken and dumplings.

Every time she visited, Grandma would make her specialty item—her famous tea cakes. Grandma's tea cakes were cookies made from scratch and were a big hit with our family. To this end, I have come to associate tea cakes with grandmothers. I honestly thought this was a cookie only my grandmother made, until much later in life when I found recipes for them in most of my cookbooks.

PATRICIA GAINES

83

I will open my mouth in parables,
I will utter hidden things, things from of old—
what we have heard and known,
what our fathers have told us.
We will not hide them from their children;
we will tell the next generation the praiseworthy
deeds of the LORD, his power, and the wonders
he has done.

PSALM 78:2–4

Surely now in my latter years I'll be able to put to good use what wisdom I have accumulated. Instead I have been going through one of the most intense learning periods of my life, especially in connection with our children and grandchildren.

I love being a grandmother. Not since I was a small girl have I had so much fun. Not only that, I have learned volumes about the delight of living in the kingdom of God while still on this earth.

CATHERINE MARSHALL

Taste and see that the L$_{ORD}$ is good.

P$_{SALM}$ 34:8

I will tell of the kindnesses of the L$_{ORD}$,
the deeds for which he is to be praised,
according to all the L$_{ORD}$ has done for us—
yes, the many good things he has done.

I$_{SAIAH}$ 63:7

Be at rest once more, O my soul,
for the L$_{ORD}$ has been good to you.

P$_{SALM}$ 116:7

Until I was nine years old, my family lived on the bottom floor of a large three-story house, with my grandparents and various aunts, uncles, and cousins living on the second and third floors. Needless to say, I spent a good bit of time in my Nana's home, especially on the days that she'd bake her wonderful dark chocolate cake!

PHYLLIS DUFFY

My widowed grandmother had ten children, thirty-four grandchildren, and little money. But at Christmas she always brought us special treats: stuffed dates rolled in sugar, and her special pudding with cranberry sauce. Her simple gifts made us feel special.

DWR

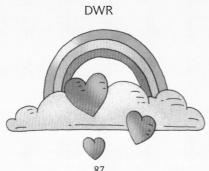

The birth of a grandchild is a wonderful and exciting event! That wonder and excitement continues throughout life.

TOM POTTS

Becoming a grandmother is wonderful. One moment you're just a mother. The next you are all-wise and prehistoric.

PAM BROWN

How does it feel to be a grandmother? A little odd? It seems quite crazy that your baby should be sitting there with a baby of her own on her lap. But good. A sort of bonus.

PAM BROWN

Ten Reasons for a Grandma

1. Grandmas always show unconditional love.

2. Who else would even think of boasting about you to a total stranger.

3. Moms don't always respond positively to: "Can I have that? Can I? CAN I?"

4. No one else's place is more fun to visit.

5. Hearing neat stories about the good old days without reading a history book.

6. Nobody hugs better.

7. A grandma always knows when to put down what she is doing and just listen.

8. Grandmas always make sure to have your favorite treat on hand.

9. Grandmas know just what you want for special occasions, not what you need.

10. "Over the river and through the woods, to Aunt Mary's house we go" just doesn't have the same ring to it.

There is only one thing more exciting than becoming a grandmother ...
becoming a great-grandmother.

CHARLOTTE WYNBEEK

Holding a great-grandchild makes getting old worthwhile.

EVALYN RIKKERS

The LORD has done great things for us and we are filled with joy.

PSALM 126:3

In spite of the circumstances of my birth, I was not a mistake. My sainted great-grand-mother, who raised me from the time I was two years old, made sure I knew this crucial truth. "Baby," she said, "there was never a seed planted in a mother's womb that God didn't know about and have special plans for. You just remember that. You are somebody!"

THELMA WELLS

My great-grandmother was a sweet woman with curly white hair, sixties cat glasses, and skin like velvet. She had given up her dreams of performing in order to marry a widower with three small boys. She always hid little packages of Lifesavers in her cupboards for me to find. From her I learned about compassion and putting others first.

MOLLY DETWEILER

What a wonder to sit and hold my great-granddaughter in my arms, gaze into her eyes, and remember my daughter and granddaughter who were once my babies too but are now all grown up. Reflecting on it makes me feel very old but very proud.

CHARLOTTE WYNBEEK

Love begins at home,

and it is not how much we do

but how much love

we put in that action.

MOTHER TERESA

When it seems the world can't understand,
Your grandmother's there to hold your hand.

With her gentle words and open heart
Your grandmother shares with graceful art.

Her adoring eyes see just the best
Your grandmother will ignore the rest.

A grandmother's love means oh, so much!
Your grandmother has that magic touch.

JOYCE K. ALLEN LOGAN

The LORD bless you

and keep you;

the LORD make his face

shine upon you

and be gracious to you;

the LORD turn his face

toward you and give you peace.

NUMBERS 6:24–26

SOURCES

Braude, Jacob M. *Braude's Source Book for Speakers & Writers.* Englewood Cliffs, N.J.: Prentice Hall, 1968.

Pam Brown: From *To a Very Special Grandmother*©Helen Exley 1991. Used by permission of Exley Publications Ltd.

Brownlow, Caroline. *Grandmother.* Fort Worth, Texas: Brownlow, 1999.

Buursma, Dirk. *NIV Daylight Devotional Bible.* Grand Rapids, MI: ZondervanPublishingHouse,1988.

de Vinck, Christopher. *The Book of Moonlight.* Grand Rapids, MI: ZondervanPublishingHouse, 1998.

Dillow, Linda. *Creative Counterpart.* Nashville, TN: Thomas Nelson, Inc. 1986

Doan, Eleanor. *The Complete Speakers Sourcebook.* Grand Rapids, MI. ZondervanPublishingHouse, 1996.

Goode, Ruth. *A Book for Grandmothers.* Curtis Brown Ltd, 1976.

Graham, Ruth Bell. *It's My Turn.* Grand Rapids, MI: Fleming H. Revell, a division of Baker Book House. 1982.

Gundry, Pat. *The Zondervan Family Cookbook.* Grand Rapids, MI: ZondervanPublishingHouse, 1988

Ingram, Kristen. *I'll Ask Grandmother, She's Very Wise.* Uhrichsville, OH: Promise Press an imprint of Barbour, 1999.

Lanese, Janet. *Grandmothers Are Like Snowflakes.* New York, NY: Dell Publishing, 1996.

Marshall, Catherine. *Meeting God at Every Turn.* Grand Rapids, MI: Flemming H. Revell, a division of Baker Book House, 1980.

Mother Teresa of Calcutta. Quoted in *Journey Magazine.* Nashville, TN: Baptist Sunday School Board, November 1994.

NIV Women's Devotional Bible 2. Grand Rapids, MI: ZondervanPublishingHouse, 1995.

Potts, Tom. *98 Wise Rules for Grandpa.* Grand Rapids, MI: Baker Books a division of Baker Book House, 1994.

Price, Eugenia. *God Speaks to Women Today.* Grand Rapids, MI: ZondervanPublishingHouse, 1964.

From GRANDPARENTS by Charlie W. Shedd, copyright © 1976 by Charlie W. Shedd and The Abundance Foundation. Used by permission of Doubleday, a divison of Random House, Inc.

Stoop, Jan and Betty Southard. *The Grandmother Book.* Nashville, TN: Thomas Nelson Publishers, 1993.

Von Suttner, Bertha. Quoted in *Great Quotes from Great Women.* Celebrating Excellence, Inc. 1991.

Weaver, Frances. *The Girls with the Grandmother Faces.* Saratoga Springs, NY: 1987.

Wells, Thelma. *Outrageous Joy.* Grand Rapids, MI: ZondervanPublishingHouse, 1999.

The Women's Study Bible. Nashville, TN: Thomas Nelson, Inc. 1995.